Supply Chains
IN INFOGRAPHICS

Christina Hill

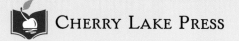
CHERRY LAKE PRESS

Published in the United States of America by Cherry Lake Publishing Group
Ann Arbor, Michigan
www.cherrylakepublishing.com

Reading Adviser: Beth Walker Gambro, MS, Ed., Reading Consultant, Yorkville, IL

Photo Credits: ©Cover, Page 1: ©TarikVision/Getty Images; Page 5: ©elenab/Shutterstock; Page 8: ©Red monkey/Shutterstock; Page 10: ©Apple, Inc./Wikimedia; Page 10: ©olesia_g/Shutterstock; Page 11: ©olesia_g/Shutterstock; Page 12: ©Mohamed Hassan/Pixabay,©OpenClipart-Vectors/Pixabay; Page 13: ©Clker-Free-Vector-Images/Pixabay, ©OpenClipart-Vectors/Pixabay; Page 16: ©Marish/Shutterstock; Page 18: ©Amanita Silvicora/Shutterstock, ©FlowerOFdestiny/Pixabay, ©Revolutionizzed/Shutterstock; Page 19: ©GoodStudio/Shutterstock, ©jedynka/Pixabay, ©OpenClipart-Vectors/Pixabay, ©Tomislav Kaučić/Pixabay; Page 23: ©John Takai/Shutterstock; Page 24: ©Mind Pixell/Shutterstock, ©valikalina/Shutterstock; Page 25: ©inspiredbythemuse/Pixabay, ©OpenClipart-Vectors/Pixabay, ©valikalina/Shutterstock; Page 26: ©AlexZel/Pixabay, ©carina/Shutterstock, ©DavidRockDesign/Pixabay, ©Mix3r/Shutterstock, ©OpenClipart-Vectors/Pixabay, ©Satheesh Sankaran/Pixabay; Page 27: ©Mix3r/Shutterstock; Page 28: ©Mind Pixell/Shutterstock; Page 29: ©Clker-Free-Vector-Images/Pixabay, ©Wise ant/Shutterstock; Page 30: ©Clker-Free-Vector-Images/Pixabay, ©George Mutambuka/Pixabay, ©iKandy/Shutterstock, ©monique_hernandez/Pixabay, ©OpenClipart-Vectors/Pixabay, ©Satheesh Sankaran/Pixabay, ©Werner Moser/Pixabay

Cherry Lake Press is an imprint of Cherry Lake Publishing Group.

Library of Congress Cataloging-in-Publication Data
Names: Hill, Christina, author.
Title: Supply chains in infographics / Christina Hill.
Description: Ann Arbor, Michigan : Cherry Lake Press, [2023] | Series: Econo-graphics | Includes bibliographical references and index. | Audience: Ages 9-13 | Audience: Grades 4-6 | Summary: "A supply chain is a network of people who work together across the globe to create a product that reaches a consumer. In this book, readers will learn about the complexities of supply chains and the factors that affect them. Real-world examples of supply chains are also presented, including facts about pandemic-era impacts. Colorful and clear graphics, such as maps, charts, and infographics, give readers an alternative to text-heavy sources. Action-based activities will leave students with an understanding of how supply chains work. This book also includes a glossary, index, suggested reading and websites, and a bibliography"-- Provided by publisher.
Identifiers: LCCN 2022016889 (print) | LCCN 2022016890 (ebook) | ISBN 9781668909935 (hardcover) | ISBN 9781668911532 (paperback) | ISBN 9781668914717 (pdf)
Subjects: LCSH: Business logistics--Juvenile literature.
Classification: LCC HD38.5 .H553 2023 (print) | LCC HD38.5 (ebook) | DDC 658.7--dc23/eng/20220413
LC record available at https://lccn.loc.gov/2022016889
LC ebook record available at https://lccn.loc.gov/2022016890

Cherry Lake Publishing Group would like to acknowledge the work of the Partnership for 21st Century Learning, a Network of Battelle for Kids. Please visit *http://www.battelleforkids.org/networks/p21* for more information.

Printed in the United States of America

Before embracing a career as an author, **Christina Hill** received a bachelor's degree in English from the University of California, Irvine, and a graduate degree in literature from California State University, Long Beach. When she is not writing about various subjects from sports to economics, Christina can be found hiking, mastering yoga handstands, or curled up with a classic novel. Christina lives in sunny Southern California with her husband, two sons, and beloved dog, Pepper Riley.

CONTENTS

What Is a Supply Chain?

A **supply chain** is a network of people, equipment, and technology working together to produce and **distribute** goods. There are many links in a supply chain. These links include **raw materials**, producers, warehouses, shipping companies, and stores. The goods and services move from link to link until they reach the customers.

Key Supply Chain Links

SUPPLIER
This is the start of the chain. It includes the raw materials used to make the goods.

PRODUCER
This is the factory where the goods are made.

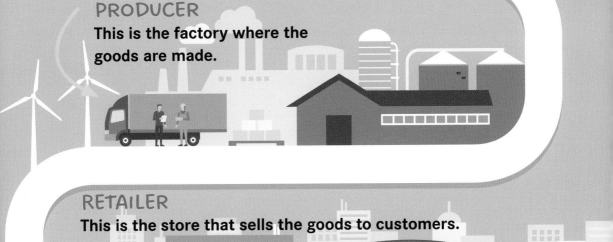

RETAILER
This is the store that sells the goods to customers.

CUSTOMER
The customer buys the goods, and the chain starts all over again.

CHAPTER 1

Types of Supply Chains

Some supply chains are simple and move in a straight line. Goods flow directly from supplier to producer to **consumer**. Other chains are not so simple. They involve a web of different suppliers and producers all working together to reach the end product. The goal of a successful supply chain is to meet the **demand** of customers quickly and at the right price.

SERVICE

Getting the right items to the right customers at the right time and cost improves customer satisfaction.

CASH

Companies must keep large amounts of raw materials or finished goods on hand to turn into cash quickly, if needed.

COST

Keeping the cost of production down is important. Producers can buy supplies in large amounts at a lower cost.

Six Types of Supply Chains

CONTINUOUS FLOW MODEL
Made for a continuous flow of goods to meet a steady customer demand (e.g., PepsiCo)

FAST MODEL
Made for goods that are very popular but only for a short time, such as the latest sneaker fad (e.g., Nike)

EFFICIENT MODEL
Made for goods that have a lot of competition because there are many brands making the same type of product; the goal is to reduce costs throughout the supply chain to help make a profit (e.g., General Mills)

AGILE MODEL
Made for goods that are unpredictable and always changing, such as trending fashion (e.g., ZARA)

FLEXIBLE MODEL
Made for companies that produce goods in large amounts when demand is high (such as school supplies in fall) but also small amounts when demand is low (e.g., Staples)

CUSTOM CONFIGURED MODEL
Made to allow for customer personalization (such as names and initials) of the goods (e.g., L.L. Bean)

2022, IDB

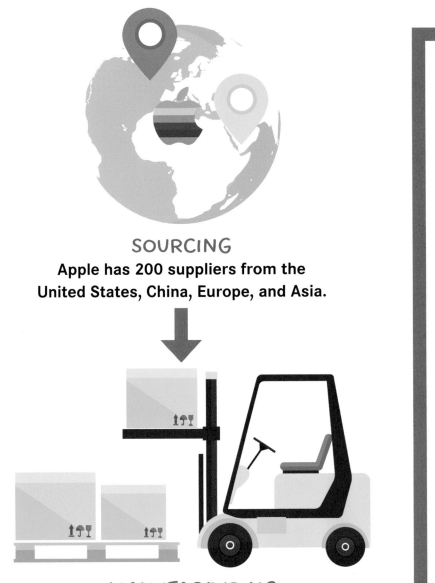

SOURCING
Apple has 200 suppliers from the United States, China, Europe, and Asia.

MANUFACTURING
All supplies are sent to a factory in China. Apple makes sure that their products are lightweight and in small packages.

WAREHOUSING

Products are either delivered to a main warehouse in California or directly to customer homes. The inventory on hand is low (about as much as can be sold in a week).

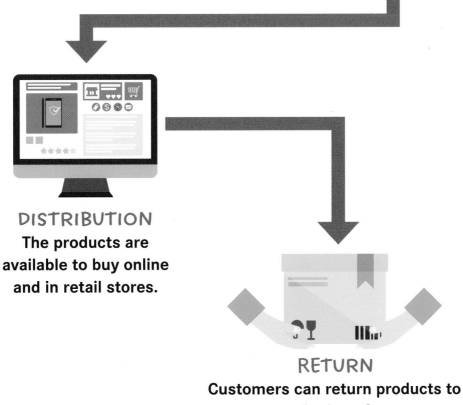

DISTRIBUTION

The products are available to buy online and in retail stores.

RETURN

Customers can return products to stores or recycle them for newer ones.

2020, Trade Gecko; 2021, Investopedia

MATERIALS

McDonald's grows its own lettuce, tomatoes, and potatoes. It raises its own cattle too.

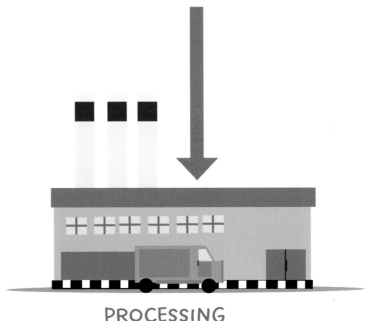

PROCESSING

All food products are processed in McDonald's factories and at the company's own high standards.

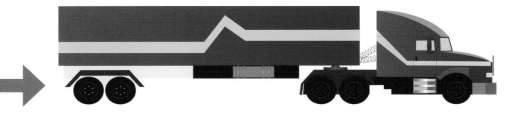

TRANSPORTATION

McDonald's transports its food in its own trucks.

RESTAURANTS

McDonald's restaurants own their buildings and land.

2019, Box Around the World; 2022, McDonald's

Fast Facts

- McDonald's has a successful **vertical integration** supply chain. This means they own or control all the parts of their supply chain.

- Customers are satisfied because their food is the same quality around the world.

- McDonald's serves more than 69 million customers every day in 39,000 restaurants.

- McDonald's has at least 1 restaurant in 118 countries and territories worldwide.

CHAPTER 2

Supply Chain Management

Supply chain management oversees the flow of goods and services through the supply chain.

This helps companies reduce costs and deliver products to the consumer faster. Good supply chain management makes sure that all parts of the chain are working correctly. The job of a supply chain manager is to reduce costs and avoid **shortages** or problems in the flow.

Five Parts of Supply Chain Management

PLAN
What materials are needed? Will they be local or brought in from another country?

SOURCE
Which supplier is right for product materials and offers the best price?

MAKE
Who can create, put together, and package the materials into goods?

DELIVER
How should the finished goods be delivered to keep **lead times** as short as possible?

RETURN
What will the return policy be? How can customers return unwanted or broken items?

THE HISTORY OF DELIVERING GOODS IN THE UNITED STATES

1800s	Deliveries of local goods are made by foot or by wagon.
1860	The Pony Express quickly delivers goods on horses across the country.
1869	The Transcontinental Railroad is completed. It covers 1,907 miles (3,069 kilometers) across the United States, transporting goods even in the cold winter months.
1907	UPS starts delivering packages locally, using bikes.
1920s	Automobile production makes shipping goods across the country faster.
1939	Cargo planes with rear-loading ramps help transport large packages with ease.
1970s	Big 18-wheel trucks become a standard shipping method. Refrigerated trucks allow food to stay fresher over long distances.

Transport Factors to Consider

COST
A $1,000 air shipment will cost only $200 by sea.

LOCATION
Is it local or global?

LEAD TIME
Airplanes are the fastest choice for long distances. Ships can take several weeks to reach the same location.

LIMITATIONS
Do the goods need to be kept cold? Are the goods too large to fit in a truck?

AVAILABILITY
What if weather slows road travel or cancels flights?

PLANET HEALTH
Airplanes create 44 times more carbon dioxide than ships do, making them a less Earth-friendly choice.

2021, Customodal

Fair Trade and Supply Chains

Fair trade is a global group of producers, businesses, and customers. They push for human rights, fair **wages**, and Earth-friendly practices in their supply chains.

Fair trade coffee sells 5 times faster than other coffee.

In 2018, fair trade products were $11.4 billion in global sales.

More than 80% of the world's fair trade cotton comes from India.

Fair Trade Certified Products

HOME GOODS

Target, Pottery Barn, and West Elm offer fair trade furniture and home decor.

CHOCOLATE

Annie's Homegrown, Ben & Jerry's, and Larabar use fair trade chocolate.

COFFEE

Kicking Horse, Marley Coffee, and Starbucks offer fair trade coffee beans.

CLOTHING

Patagonia and Universal Thread offer fair trade apparel.

2022, Fair Trade Certified

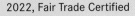

DESIGN
The United States provides the software for the microchip design.

MATERIALS
Silicon is mined in the United States. It is processed in Japan and South Korea.

2 EQUIPMENT
The equipment is made in the United States, Japan, and Europe.

4 MANUFACTURING
Microchips are made and packaged in Taiwan and Malaysia. Then they are assembled into smartphones in China.

2021, Boston Consulting Group

CHAPTER 3

Supply Chain Disruptions

Many things can **disrupt** a supply chain and cause the links in the chain to break. This is why supply chain management is so important. Throughout history, natural disasters have caused many supply chain disruptions. In 2020, the global COVID-19 pandemic destroyed supply chains across different industries. Store shelves were empty. Lead times for deliveries were long.

Natural Disasters and Supply Chains

- Hurricane Sandy struck New York in October 2012, destroying many supply chains.

- Oil tankers were blocked from arriving at port.

- 8.5 million people lost power.

- Power outages led to a fuel shortage.

- Delivery trucks were used to provide emergency aid.

- Total cost of the hurricane was $65 billion in economic damages.

2013, USA Today

When the Supply Chain Breaks

Hurricane Katrina wipes out power lines and transportation routes, disrupting many supply chains. Most companies choose to wait for the port to be restored. Why? Because it would take 15 railcars or 60 semi-trucks to carry the same amount of goods as 1 ship.

2005

2007

Boeing's supplier of bolts for their 787 Dreamliner planes fails. Boeing temporarily buys bolts from local hardware stores to fix the broken supply chain.

An earthquake and tsunami in Japan shut down a chemical plant. It is the only factory that makes paint used by U.S. car companies Ford and Chrysler. The companies delay production and offer cars only in colors that don't need the special paint.

2011

2014

The movie *Frozen* makes $1.2 billion at the box office. But Disney did not plan for the huge success. Toy shelves are emptied instantly, and the company scrambles to increase their supply. Fans are disappointed in the long wait times for restocked products.

2005, CFO; 2020, TechTarget; 2021, Disney

The 2020 Supply Chain Fail of Toilet Paper

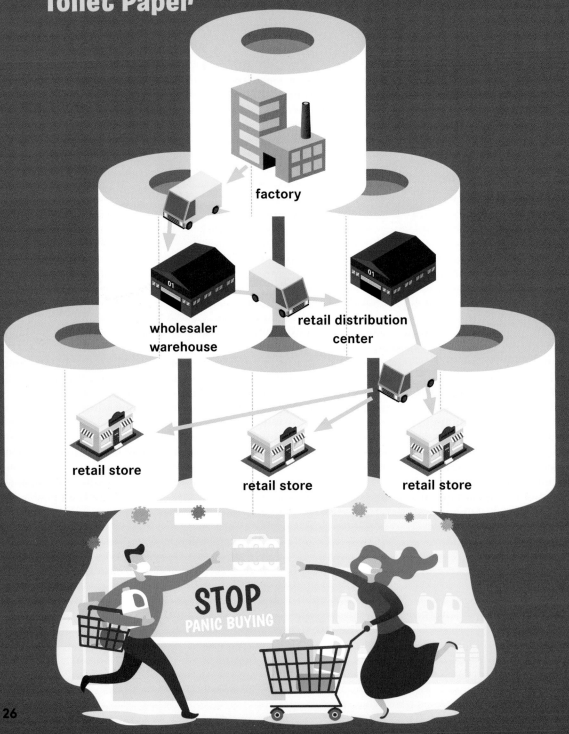

factory

wholesaler warehouse

retail distribution center

retail store

retail store

retail store

STOP PANIC BUYING

Because of the COVID-19 pandemic, stores across the world had no toilet paper left on their shelves.

Toilet paper runs on a simple and efficient supply chain. What happened?

Consumer demand was so high that there was no way the supply chain could meet it.

On March 12, 2020, toilet paper sales rose 734% compared with the same day in 2019.

By March 23, 2020, 70% of U.S. stores and online sites had no toilet paper left to sell.

2020, Forbes

Supply Chain Fails at the Shipping Ports

The Port of Los Angeles, California, handles 17% of incoming cargo sent by sea to the United States.

The COVID-19 pandemic created an increased demand for goods, but there was a shortage of workers.

A mass of ships was stuck, waiting to unload.

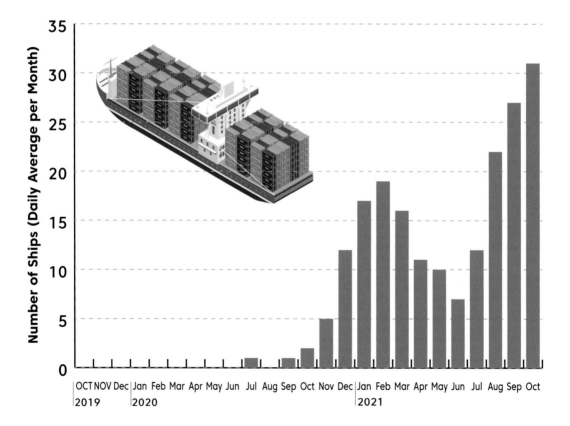

2121, American Farm Bureau Federation; 2021, Port of Los Angeles

Supply Chains of the Future

Artificial intelligence, or AI, will be able to predict supply chain issues and fix them.

Robots can lift, carry, and deliver heavy packages.

AI in the supply chain market is predicted to grow 42.9% by 2023.

AI can fill in areas where there are human worker shortages, such as truck drivers.

Self-driving vehicles can deliver goods.

HANDLE WITH CARE

2021, Forbes; 2021, Infoholic Research

Activity

Become a Supply Chain Manager

Your mom tells you that you can make cereal bar treats at home for the school bake sale. Use the supply chain below to help you manage your tasks.

RAW MATERIALS
butter, cereal, marshmallows

SUPPLIER
grocery store

TRANSPORTATION
Dad's car

PRODUCTION
you in your family's kitchen

TRANSPORTATION
your bike

RETAIL
the school bake sale

CUSTOMERS
students and families

1. How would your supply chain change if the grocery store didn't have cereal?

2. How would your supply chain change if your bike got a flat tire on the way to deliver the goods to school?

3. What do you think is the most important link in this supply chain? Explain your answer.

Learn More

Books

Jones, Kari. *A Fair Deal: Shopping for Social Justice.* Custer, WA: Orca Book Publishers, 2022.

Ventura, Marne. *Supply and Demand.* Minneapolis, MN: Cody Koala, an imprint of Pop!, 2019.

Websites

Ducksters: Money and Finance: Economics
https://www.ducksters.com/money/economics.php

EconEdLink: Supply Chain Video
https://www.econedlink.org/resources/supply-chain-video

Bibliography

Katzman, Rebecca. "A Look at the Economy." March 12, 2020. https://www.timeforkids.com/g56/coronavirus-look-at-economy

NFK Editors. "World Struggles with Supply Chain Problems." October 20, 2021. https://newsforkids.net/articles/2021/10/20/world-struggles-with-supply-chain-problems

Semuels, Alana. "How American Shoppers Broke the Supply Chain." November 2, 2021. https://time.com/6112491/supply-chain-shopping

Glossary

consumer (kuhn-SOO-mur) a person who buys goods and services

demand (dih-MAND) the desire to purchase goods and services

disrupt (dis-RUHPT) to stop the normal flow of things

distribute (dihs-TRIB-yoot) to give out

lead times (LEED TYMZ) the times between supply chain starts and the end product deliveries

raw materials (RAW meh-TEE-ree-uhlz) the basic things that can be used to make or create something

shortages (SHOR-dij-ez) when there is not enough of something that is needed

supply chain (suh-PLY CHAYN) the system of how goods or services are produced and distributed to consumers

vertical integration (VUR-tih-kuhl in-teh-GRAY-shuhn) a business model where companies own most of the links in their supply chain

wages (WAYJ-ez) an amount of money that a worker is paid based on the time worked

Index